LIFE'S LITTLE BOOK OF WISDOM FOR
Kids

© 2008 by Barbour Publishing, Inc.

ISBN 978-1-59789-961-1

Scripture quotations marked NIV are taken from the HOLY BIBLE, NEW INTERNATIONAL VERSION®. NIV®. Copyright © 1973, 1978, 1984 by International Bible Society. Used by permission of Zondervan. All rights reserved.

Scripture quotations marked MSG are from *THE MESSAGE.* Copyright © by Eugene H. Peterson 1993, 1994, 1995, 1996, 2000, 2001, 2002. Used by permission of NavPress Publishing Group.

Published by Barbour Publishing, Inc., P.O. Box 719, Uhrichsville, Ohio 44683, www.barbourbooks.com

Our mission is to publish and distribute inspirational products offering exceptional value and biblical encouragement to the masses.

Printed in China.

LIFE'S LITTLE BOOK OF
WISDOM FOR
Kids

BARBOUR
PUBLISHING

Trust God from the bottom of your heart.

Proverbs 3:5 MSG

Don't forget to
say your prayers.

LOVE YOUR BROTHER AND SISTER,
EVEN WHEN THEY DON'T DESERVE IT.

God is like a shield that protects you. Tell Him today how much you love Him for keeping you safe.

Follow your dreams.

CAST ALL YOUR ANXIETY ON HIM
BECAUSE HE CARES FOR YOU.

1 PETER 5:7 NIV

More is not always better.

WHEN YOU LAUGH,
LAUGH HARD AND LOUD.

Keep trying.

DON'T WAIT FOR YOUR BIRTHDAY OR
FOR A HOLIDAY—CELEBRATE TODAY!

{Jesus said,} "If you remain in me and my words remain in you, ask whatever you wish, and it will be given you."

John 15:7 niv

No matter how small you are,
God hears your prayers.

Don't give someone else a nickname you wouldn't want.

Learn when to be still—
and when to party!

DO SOMETHING GOOD
FOR SOMEONE IN SECRET.

"For God so loved the world
that he gave his one and only Son,
that whoever believes in him shall
not perish but have eternal life."

John 3:16 NIV

Don't spend time worrying about things that probably won't happen.

ASK AS MANY QUESTIONS AS IT TAKES
TO FIND OUT THE COMPLETE ANSWER.

THANK YOUR MOM AND DAD FOR
DINNER—EVEN WHEN IT'S JUST LEFTOVERS.

If you want to make friends,
be a friend to others.

IF WE CONFESS OUR SINS,
HE IS FAITHFUL AND JUST AND WILL
FORGIVE US OUR SINS AND PURIFY US
FROM ALL UNRIGHTEOUSNESS.

1 JOHN 1:9 NIV

Hang on tight.

BE COURAGEOUS!
TRY A FOOD YOU'VE
NEVER TASTED BEFORE.

Wear your favorite outfit when you're feeling down.

GOD'S LOVE FOR YOU IS SO BIG,
YOU CAN'T MEASURE IT.

Do something good.

Psalm 34:14 MSG

SOMETIMES A LITTLE HUG
CAN HELP THE BIGGEST HURTS.

It's impossible to take back mean words, no matter how hard you try.

As fun as it sounds,
a haircut you give yourself
is *never* a good idea.

READ YOUR FAVORITE BOOK UNTIL
YOU HAVE IT MEMORIZED.

Obey God's Word.

Share your favorite
snack with a friend.

Playing in the rain is sometimes more fun than playing in the sunshine.

NEVER LET A GOOD
OPPORTUNITY PASS YOU BY.

ASK YOUR GRANDPARENTS WHAT IT
WAS LIKE WHEN THEY WERE KIDS.

{Jesus said,} "I am
the light of the world."

John 8:12 niv

You are in
God's hands.

WHEN SOMEONE YOU KNOW
FEELS DOWN, SOMETIMES THE
FOUR BEST WORDS TO SAY ARE,
"I BELIEVE IN YOU."

Pouters usually play
by themselves.

When you feel like singing,
share your song loudly!

You can be sure that God will take care of everything you need.

Philippians 4:19 msg

WHEN ONE DOOR CLOSES. . .
ANOTHER DOOR OPENS.

Don't simply walk
if you can skip.

Y OU DON'T HAVE TO BE
FIRST EVERY TIME.

When God speaks,
listen.

GOD IS FAITHFUL; HE WILL NOT LET YOU BE TEMPTED BEYOND WHAT YOU CAN BEAR. BUT WHEN YOU ARE TEMPTED, HE WILL ALSO PROVIDE A WAY OUT SO THAT YOU CAN STAND UP UNDER IT.

1 CORINTHIANS 10:13 NIV

DON'T EVER BE AFRAID,
BECAUSE GOD PROMISES TO PROTECT YOU
AND LOVE YOU–ALWAYS.

Invite the new kid to play with you during recess.

GROWING A PLANT IS A GOOD WAY
TO SHOW YOU'RE RESPONSIBLE
ENOUGH FOR A PET.

There's no such thing
as too many friends.

PUT YOUR ENTIRE TRUST
IN THE MASTER JESUS.
THEN YOU'LL LIVE AS YOU
WERE MEANT TO LIVE.

ACTS 16:31 MSG

If you don't have
something nice to say,
don't say anything at all.

When you have
something nice to say,
say it!

God loves you more than
you love your favorite toy.

IF YOU CAN'T SING,
PLAY AN INSTRUMENT.

"Do not store up for
yourselves treasures on earth. . . .
But store up for yourselves
treasures in heaven. . . .
For where your treasure is,
there your heart will be also."

Matthew 6:19-21 niv

When someone hurts your feelings, forgive him. It will make God happy.

LYING IN THE GRASS AND
LOOKING UP IN THE SKY IS
MORE ENTERTAINING THAN TV.

Even when you feel lonely,
God is with you.

Let Jesus change
your heart.

AND WE KNOW THAT IN ALL
THINGS GOD WORKS FOR THE
GOOD OF THOSE WHO LOVE HIM.

ROMANS 8:28 NIV

The greatest love
comes from God.

It's good to help others,
even before they ask for help.

EVEN A GOURMET CHEF STARTS
OUT MAKING MUD PIES.

DOING SOMETHING AS A TEAM
IS OFTEN MORE REWARDING
THAN DOING IT BY YOURSELF.

"DON'T PICK ON PEOPLE, JUMP ON THEIR FAILURES, CRITICIZE THEIR FAULTS—UNLESS, OF COURSE, YOU WANT THE SAME TREATMENT. . . . BE EASY ON PEOPLE; YOU'LL FIND LIFE A LOT EASIER. . . . GIVING, NOT GETTING, IS THE WAY. GENEROSITY BEGETS GENEROSITY."

LUKE 6:37-38 MSG

Love others.

It is better to admit a mistake than to hide it.

*H*ANDMADE PRESENTS ARE THE
BEST KIND TO GIVE—AND TO GET.

God is here, even when
you can't feel Him.

[Jesus said,] "The person who loves me will be loved by my Father, and I will love him and make myself plain to him."

John 14:21 MSG

Look forward to tomorrow's opportunities.

REMEMBER TO THANK
THE LUNCH LADY.

WATCHING A SCARY MOVIE SEEMS LIKE
A GOOD IDEA UNTIL YOU HAVE TO
GO TO BED IN THE DARK.

Giving gifts feels better than getting them.

Read God's Word.

EVEN IF YOU MAKE BIG MISTAKES,
GOD WILL FORGIVE YOU.
ALL YOU NEED TO DO IS ASK HIM!

IF YOU WANT SOMETHING TO HAPPEN, DON'T JUST TALK ABOUT IT–DO IT!

DON'T WAIT TO TELL SOMEONE YOU LOVE THEM.

Something that looks good isn't always the best choice.

Fix your attention on God.
You'll be changed
from the inside out.

Romans 12:2 msg

WHEN YOU'RE NOT SURE WHAT TO DO,
ASK GOD.

Ask for help if
you need it.

DON'T WISH AWAY YOUR
TODAY FOR TOMORROW.

Remember to
wash your hands.

CHILDREN, OBEY YOUR PARENTS
IN EVERYTHING,
FOR THIS PLEASES THE LORD.

COLOSSIANS 3:20 NIV

PASS ON THE KINDNESSES
OTHERS SHOW YOU.

IF YOU START YOUR MORNING TALKING TO GOD, HE WILL GUIDE YOU EVERY MINUTE OF THE REST OF THE DAY.

Be a good
friend to others.

Never doubt yourself.

BE CHEERFUL NO MATTER WHAT;
PRAY ALL THE TIME; THANK GOD
NO MATTER WHAT HAPPENS.
THIS IS THE WAY GOD WANTS YOU
WHO BELONG TO CHRIST JESUS TO LIVE.

1 THESSALONIANS 5:16-18 MSG

Pray for others.

GOD'S MOST WONDERFUL CREATION IS YOU!

You don't have to grow up
on the inside.

WHEN YOU ARE WEAK,
GOD WILL BE YOUR STRENGTH.

BE KIND AND COMPASSIONATE TO
ONE ANOTHER, FORGIVING EACH OTHER,
JUST AS IN CHRIST GOD FORGAVE YOU.

EPHESIANS 4:32 NIV

BELIEVE IN YOUR HEART THAT
GOD WILL DO WHAT HE SAYS—
BECAUSE HE ALWAYS WILL!

Be thankful for
everything you have.

DON'T LET FEARS STAND
IN THE WAY OF YOUR DREAMS.

Let Jesus be your
best friend.

Jesus replied: " 'Love the Lord your God with all your heart and with all your soul and with all your mind.' This is the first and greatest commandment."

Matthew 22:37-38 NIV

THANK YOUR PARENTS FOR
ALL THEY DO FOR YOU.

LOOK FOR THE GOOD IN EVERYTHING AND EVERYONE, AND YOU WILL FIND IT.

ONLY GOD CAN MAKE SOMETHING
AS BIG AND AMAZING AS THE MILLIONS
OF TWINKLING STARS IN THE NIGHT SKY.

Don't do something just because everyone else is doing it.

LISTEN FOR GOD'S VOICE
IN EVERYTHING YOU DO,
EVERYWHERE YOU GO;
HE'S THE ONE WHO WILL
KEEP YOU ON TRACK.

PROVERBS 3:6 MSG

Always tell the truth—
no ifs, ands, or buts!

ASK GOD TO HELP YOU
SOLVE YOUR PROBLEMS.

Have an "I can" attitude.

ALL MUSIC OF PRAISE IS
BEAUTIFUL TO GOD'S EARS.

Do your best.

COLOSSIANS 3:23 MSG

DON'T BE AFRAID TO
TRY SOMETHING NEW.
YOU MIGHT JUST ENJOY IT!

Be confident.

Choose to be
a good person.

Say it, whisper it, or sing it;
make sure you say "I love you" often.

GIVE THANKS TO THE LORD,
FOR HE IS GOOD;
HIS LOVE ENDURES FOREVER.

PSALM 107:1 NIV

Be a good neighbor.

Learn from
your mistakes.

With God as your helper,
you can face anyone or
anything and not be afraid.

Give big bear hugs.

THE LORD. . .DELIGHTS IN MEN
WHO ARE TRUTHFUL.

PROVERBS 12:22 NIV

Sometimes it's okay
to say no.

No matter how big a problem is,
it's never bigger than God.

Sing a new song.

You're never too grown up
to hold a friend's hand.

"BAD COMPANY RUINS
GOOD MANNERS."

1 CORINTHIANS 15:33 MSG

Celebrate with your friends
when they're happy.

GOD'S LOVE IS MORE PRICELESS
THAN BURIED TREASURE.

Every day is a gift—
don't waste it!

God is never too
busy to hear you.

KEEP YOUR TONGUE FROM EVIL
AND YOUR LIPS FROM SPEAKING LIES.

PSALM 34:13 NIV

Never do anything that will embarrass your mother!

Renée Sattler

SPEND TIME LAUGHING AND
PLAYING WITH YOUR FAMILY.

Expect a surprise
every day.

GOD HAS MORE THOUGHTS ABOUT YOU
THAN THERE ARE GRAINS OF SAND.

GOD IS A SAFE PLACE TO HIDE,
READY TO HELP WHEN WE NEED HIM.

PSALM 46:1 MSG

THANK GOD FOR LISTENING
TO YOUR PRAYERS.

.

SHOW YOUR LOVE FOR OTHERS
THROUGH YOUR ACTIONS
AND YOUR WORDS.

Tell others when you are praying for them.

When you are a helper,
you are sharing God's love.

WHEN SOMEONE ELSE IS TALKING,
DON'T INTERRUPT.

Say "please" and
"thank you."

ANGER USUALLY DOES NOT
SOLVE PROBLEMS—
IT MAKES THEM WORSE.

Pets are God's gifts to us to care for and love.

DON'T BLAME SOMEONE ELSE
FOR A MISTAKE YOU MADE.

GOD LOVES IT WHEN THE GIVER
DELIGHTS IN THE GIVING.

2 CORINTHIANS 9:7 MSG

Don't be afraid to be different from others.

When you share with others,
you share with Jesus.

You are more precious to God than all the diamonds in the world!

Your words have the power
to make others feel happy or sad.
Choose to say the ones
that bring happiness.

{Jesus said,} "Love one another."

John 13:34 NIV

Encourage others.

Do your chores without complaining.

Thank God for
your talents.

IT'S OKAY TO BE PROUD OF
YOURSELF FOR A JOB WELL DONE.

Come near to God and he will come near to you.

JAMES 4:8 NIV

BE QUICK TO SAY "I'M SORRY"
WHEN YOU HURT SOMEONE ELSE.

TEAMWORK BRINGS OUT
THE BEST IN EVERYONE.

Never say
"I can't."

DECIDE THAT TODAY IS
THE BEST DAY OF THE YEAR.

Children, do what your parents tell you.

EPHESIANS 6:1 MSG

Smile.
You'll give others
a reason to be joyful.

TAKE TIME TO LISTEN TO WHAT
OTHERS ARE REALLY SAYING.

LEARN FROM YOUR FAILURES,
BUT NEVER FORGET THEM.

Encourage at least one person every day.

Let us not become weary in doing good.

Galatians 6:9 niv

Dance like no one is watching!

RENÉE SATTLER

Celebrate your
achievements!

TRY TO FIND BEAUTY IN
GOD'S CREATION EVERY DAY.

*H*ELP DO A HOUSEHOLD CHORE
WITHOUT BEING ASKED.

TELL YOUR NEIGHBOR THE TRUTH.
IN CHRIST'S BODY WE'RE ALL
CONNECTED TO EACH OTHER, AFTER ALL.
WHEN YOU LIE TO OTHERS,
YOU END UP LYING TO YOURSELF.

EPHESIANS 4:25 MSG

ALWAYS KEEP
YOUR PROMISES.

Don't be afraid
to be wrong.

Be positive.

PUSH YOURSELF TO DO
JUST A LITTLE BIT MORE
THAN YOU THINK YOU CAN.

L<small>ET'S NOT JUST TALK ABOUT LOVE;
LET'S PRACTICE REAL LOVE. . . .</small>
F<small>OR</small> G<small>OD IS GREATER THAN OUR WORRIED
HEARTS AND KNOWS MORE ABOUT US
THAN WE DO OURSELVES.</small>

1 J<small>OHN</small> 3:18 <small>MSG</small>

No matter how others
may treat you,
God always loves you.

READ A NEW BOOK.

Be yourself.

TAKE RESPONSIBILITY FOR YOUR
ACTIONS AND DECISIONS.

DON'T TALK DIRTY OR SILLY.
THAT KIND OF TALK
DOESN'T FIT OUR STYLE.

EPHESIANS 5:3 MSG

Share.

DECIDE ON A GOAL
AND GO FOR IT!

SEEK THE TRUTH AND IT
WILL SET YOU FREE.

Shout for joy!

Don't push your way to the front;
don't sweet-talk your way
to the top. Put yourself aside,
and help others get ahead.

Philippians 2:3-4 msg

With God's help, you can do anything!